Noirmot v. Rosemary, the U.S. Supreme Court Transcript of Record with Supporting Pleadings

JACOB LOUIS MOREWITZ

Noirmot v. Rosemary, the
Petition / JACOB LOUIS MOREWITZ / 1925 / 1092 / 271 U.S. 670 / 46 S.Ct. 484 / 70 L.Ed. 1143 / 4-2-1926

Noirmot v. Rosemary, the U.S. Supreme Court Transcript of Record with Supporting Pleadings

Table of Contents

Supreme Court of the United States

OCTOBER TERM, 1925.

No. 10926  11

WILLIAM NOIRMOT, J. OLSEN, PEDER HANSEN,
J. WINDEHL AND M. DERRANE,

Libellants-Petitioners,

—*versus*—

SCHOONER "ROSEMARY", CHARLES J. DENE-
CHAUD, OWNER, AND W. N. BURBIDGE, MASTER,

Libellees-Respondents.

PETITION AND BRIEF IN SUPPORT OF APPLICATION FOR WRIT OF CERTIORARI.

JACOB LOUIS MOREWITZ,
Proctor for Libellants-Petitioners.

INDEX

The Statutes Involved

Authorities Cited

Petition for Certiorari.

TO THE
SUPREME COURT OF THE
UNITED STATES OF AMERICA

The petition of WILLIAM NOIRMOT, et al., for a Writ of Certiorari, directed to the Circuit Court of Appeals for the Fourth Circuit, to bring before the Supreme Court the case of

WILLIAM NOIRMOT, J. OLSEN, PEDER HANSEN,
J. WINDEHL AND M. DERRANE,

Libellants-Petitioners

—against—

SCHOONER "ROSEMARY", CHARLES J. DENECHAUD, OWNER,
AND W. N. BURBIDGE, MASTER,

Libellees-Respondents.

Your petitioners respectfully show to this Court as follows:

1. Your petitioners, late members of the crew of the American Schooner "ROSEMARY" filed their libel in the District Court for the Eastern District of Virginia on the 30th day of October, 1924, alleging three separate and distinct causes of action (R 2-6, 79).

The first cause asserted William Noirmot's claim, under Section 33 of the "Merchant Marine Act of 1920" for personal injuries sustained in falling from a defective ladder which crumbled under his weight while he was standing on it in the discharge of his duties on the vessel, and for the negligent failure of the respondents to furnish said Noirmot with proper medical cure and treatment after he had sustained said injuries (R 2-3). Both of these issues were decided in Noirmot's favor by the trial court and the Circuit Court of Appeals for the Fourth Circuit (R 79-80, 96), whose opinions are reported in 9 F. (2d) 980 and 982, respectively.

The second cause of action set up Noirmot's claim for $108.18 earned wages, at the rate of $80.00 per month, in addition to certain overtime, and the statutory allowances alleged to be due, under Rev. St. 4568 & 4612, as extra wages, on account of the shortage and bad quality of rations furnished on the voyage (R 4, and District Court's opinion, R 79).

The third cause of action re-asserted and amplified, on behalf of all of your petitioners (R 4-6, 79), the allegations previously made by Noirmot with respect to the aforesaid shortages and bad quality of food, and also set forth that all of the petitioners claimed 'waiting time' under Rev. St. 4529, as amended, of two days' pay for each day that their respective wages, due for work done or by way of extra allowances, as aforesaid, were wrongfully withheld.

II. That over petitioner Noirmot's objection (R 21, 61-67) the sum of $88.15 was deposited with the Shipping Commissioner at Newport News, Virginia, by said respondents, on the 23rd day of October, 1924, with instructions not to pay said sum to Noirmot, unless said petitioner would sign the statutory release, without the right of noting his protest thereon (R 28-29; 61-62; 66-67; Original Exhibits: W. L. B. No. 2 & 3) and nothing was done toward permitting Noirmot to receive *unconditionally* the money thus admitted to be due him until the 5th day of January, 1925 (R 10; 61-62; 66-67; and trial Court's opinion R 80-81), when a so-called amended libel was filed as hereinafter set forth.

That on the 21st day of November, 1924, the respondents interposed an answer (R 6-9) denying in substance the allegations of the first cause of action; denying, in respect to the second cause of action, that Noirmot had $108.18 (earned wages) due him and asserting that such sum as was due him had been deposited with the Shipping Commissioner at Newport News, Virginia, and further denying that Noirmot was entitled to any allowances for overtime, or on account of short and bad quality rations, but *admitting* 'that there was a shortage for the period of about five days' (R 8) of butter; and denying *in toto* the claims set up in Articles 7, 8 & 9, under your petitioners' third cause of action. The respondents thereafter, on the 5th day of January, 1925, filed their aforesaid amended answer, adopting the allegations contained in the original answer and *admitting* that there was then due and owing to petitioner Noirmot by said respondents $88.15 (earned wages), but insisting that said sum represented the entire amount due said Noirmot, and thereupon, for the *first time*, made a purported tender of the said sum, depositing it in the Registry of the District Court to Noirmot's credit, *without* any previous notice, and making *no effort* to take care of the accrued Court costs amounting to $232.74. By reason of the premises, Noirmot was forced to go without the $88.15 admittedly due until subsequent to January 9, 1925 (R 11-81). The indemnity then due him under Rev. Stat. 4529, *supra,* even if based on the $70.00 monthly wage paid to Boatswains, amounted to $373.33 (R 46, 101) or if calculated at the $80.00 rate stipulated in the Ship's Articles, *infra,* (R 46) would have totalled $421.33.

III. That the learned trial court awarded petitioner Noirmot on his first cause of action a total of Five Hundred Dollars ($500.00) for the personal injuries sustained by reason of the respondents' failure to furnish him with a safe place to work, and safe and suitable appliances in connection with the service, including therein the Two Hundred Dollars ($200.00) allowed said petitioner by reason of the respondent's failure to furnish him with proper medical care and cure after he was injured, but denied a recovery to any of the petitioners on the second and third causes of action set up in the libel. However, during the course of the hearing of this case before him, the trial judge *found* that the said petitioners had not been furnished with the quality (R 48-49) and quantity of food required by the Ship's Articles (p. 1 of Respondents' Exhibit W. L. B. No. 7) and Rev. St. 4568 & 4612 (R 49-51, 62, 64-66) but later, when handing down its opinion, 9 F. (2d) 980, *supra,* the court concluded that the petitioners had lost their rights on this score (R 81-82), though the respondent Master (R 8, 22, 30, 65) and the ship's cook (Shipping Commissioner's Certificate: Original Exhibit E) freely *admitted* that shortages existed during the last thirty-nine (39) days of the voyage.

IV. That with regard to Noirmot's claim under Rev. Stat. 4529 for the indemnity of two day's pay for each day his wages were withheld without sufficient cause, the trial court found that only by accepting the same *in full* of *all* of the wages *claimed* by him, could Noirmot have obtained the $88.15 admitted to be due (R 10,81), but held that, having been made an allowance for the time lost in his cure, in connection with the Two Hundred Dollars awarded (no part of which has, *as yet,* been paid Noirmot: R 80, 83-84), for the respondent's failure to more promptly furnish him with medical aid and such cure, the ship ought not to bear this loss a second time, though a finding was made that the grasp of Noirmot's hand was impaired for *six months* or more after he was injured (which in itself entitled him to *wages,* of at least $480.00, in addition to maintenance, during said period: R 51).

V. That the District Court's decree was entered on the Twenty-third day of February, 1925 (R 82), and *cross-appeals* were duly prosecuted by all the parties (R 84-87) to the Circuit Court of Appeals for the Fourth Circuit. The latter Court (R 96) on November 23rd, 1925, delivered the following *per curiam* opinion, 9 F. (2d) 982, *supra*:

"We have considered the testimony and the oral and printed arguments. We are satisfied that the amount awarded by the decree below to the libellant Noirmot is ample to cover all claims he has against the respondents or either of them. We are not prepared to say it is excessive. We believe that the learned Court below was right in holding that the other libellants had failed to establish any ground for recovery."

Thereafter and on January 12th, 1926, the said Circuit Court of Appeals denied, without opinion, the petition for rehearing that had been theretofore duly filed, on December 19th, 1925, by your petitioners (R 99-106).

VI.   The questions and propositions of law involved in this case are as follows:

1.   Was Noirmot's injured condition any justification for the purported disrating from Chief Officer to Boatswain (R 24-27; 57-59; 81)? See *Butler v. Pacific* (CCA 9) 290 Fed. 806; *Maclachlan's Law of Merchant Shipping* (6 Ed.) page 170; and *particularly* Rev. Stats. 4580 & 4581.

2.   May the wages of seamen be forfeited by the master of a vessel (R 27-29) without complying with Rev. Stat. 4290, et seq, 4550, 4596, 4597, et seq, as construed in *The Cora F. Cressy*, 131 Fed. 144; *The St. Paul*, 133 Fed. 1002; *The Ellen Little*, 246 Fed. 151; *The Elizabeth Maersk*; 258 Fed. 765; *Gordon v. U. S.*, 298 Fed. 555, 35 *CYC* 1217, et seq, & 1226-7?

3.   Did the requirement (R 28-29; 61-62; 66-67; 81) that Noirmot execute a release *in full* of all his claims before permitting him to receive the wages *admittedly due*, fail in any respect to constitute a *withholding* of said wages *without sufficient cause*, such as is denounced by Rev. Stat. 4529, as construed in *Pacific Mail S. S. Co. v Schmidt*, 241 U. S. 245 *Burns v. Davis* (CCA 1) 271 Fed. 439; *Vincent v. U. S.* (CCA 9) 272 Fed. 889; *Gerber v. Spencer* (CCA 9) 278 Fed. 886, 89-90, and in *Mandelin v. Kenncally*, 1926 A. M. C._____; 10 F. (2d) _____, which was decided in the court below by Judges Waddill, Parker and McDowell, on February 27, 1926, three months after Judges Rose,

Parker and Watkins, sitting in the *same appellate court,* had handed down, in the instant case, the per curiam opinion, above set out (R 103)?

4. The allegations regarding shortages of food having been *admitted* by respondents and the trial court having *found* the same to be true (R 8, 22, 29, 30, 49-51, 62-68) does not Rev. St. 4568 & 4612, as construed in *Billings v. Bauback* (CCA 9) 200 Fed. 523; *The Emma F. Angell,* 217 Fed. 311; *Nelson v. Patsel* (CCA 9) 232 Fed. 682; *Thompson v. Martin,* 16 App. Cas. (D. C.) 222; and *Vincent v. U. S.* (CCA 9) 272 Fed. 889, *supra,* make it the *mandatory* duty of this court to require that *all* the petitioners herein be awarded the allowances specified therein, for the respondents' failure to provide them during the last thirty-nine (39) days of the voyage, with the quality and quantity of food contracted for thereunder?

5. Having elected (R 3) to base his cause of action for personal injuries on Section 33 of the "Merchant Marine Act" of June 5th, 1920, as construed by this Court in *Panama v. Johnson,* 264 U. S. 374, was it properly held by the lower courts that Noirmot's separate cause of action, for the aforesaid *wage contract indemnity* (amounting, when the trial court's decision was handed down on February 12, 1925 (R 79) to $602.67, if based on the $80.00 monthly wage contracted for, or $527.33 if calculated at the $70.00 rate), could not be enforced because of the Two Hundred Dollars decreed him, but *still unpaid* (R 83-84), by way of *damages,* on a *prior, separate* and *distinct* cause of action, predicated on said Section 33 of said "Merchant Marine Act", for the *negligent failure* of respondents to

promptly furnish Noirmot with proper medical attention and cure after he was injured, through, what the trial court *found* to be, the respondents' negligence, (R 79-81; 96)?

6. Does the penalty of double wages, provided by R. S. 4529, apply when there is a refusal to pay *extra wages*, due under R. S. 4568, for failure to furnish proper food?

VII. And your petitioners further aver that the present case is one in which it is proper for the Court to issue a writ of certiorari, for the following reasons:

1. Because the decision appealed from, involving the interpretation of the Constitution and Statutes of the United States, is untenable, being in conflict with the applicable decisions of this Court, the Circuit Courts of Appeals for the First, Second and Ninth Circuits, the Court of Appeals for the District of Columbia, and the respective District Courts, *supra*, on the same matters.

2. Because a majority of the questions of law involved herein have not been passed upon by this Court.

3. Because the effect of the decision herein is to deny to American seamen the substantial rights granted them by Congress and to leave open to conjecture the questions submitted for adjudication.

4. Because the Statutes of the United States involved are part of highly remedial Acts, intended, in the language of Mr. Justice Sutherland, who spoke for this Court in *O'Hara v. Luckenbach*, 70 L. ed. 160, at 161, 'to safeguard the welfare of seamen as workmen'; and most of said Statutes have never been construed by this Court. See *Pacific v. Lucas*, 258 U. S. 266; *Strathearn v. Dillon*, 252 U. S. 348; *Sandberg v. McDonald*, 248 U. S. 185.

5. Because the public interests and the interests of jurisprudence require the binding decision of this Court upon each one of the questions of law involved herein.

6. Because the interests of navigation will be benefited by having this Court pass upon and determine the exact rights existing between shipowners and seamen in respect to *all* the points involved in this case.

Wherefore, petitioners pray that this Honorable Court will be pleased to grant a writ of certiorari herein, directed to the Circuit Court of Appeals for the Fourth Circuit, to bring up this case to this Court for such proceedings therein as may seem just and proper in the premises.

JACOB LOUIS MOREWITZ,
Proctor for Petitioners.

STATE OF VIRGINIA,
CITY OF NEWPORT NEWS, to-wit:

Jacob Louis Morewitz, being duly sworn, says: That he is the proctor for the petitioners herein, and that the foregoing petition is true to the best of his knowledge, information and belief.

JACOB LOUIS MOREWITZ.

Sworn to before me this
23rd day of March, 1926.
H. T. PARKER,
Notary Public.

I hereby certify that I have examined the foregoing petition, and in my opinion, the petition is well founded, and entitled to the favorable consideration of the Court.

JACOB LOUIS MOREWITZ,
Proctor for Petitioners.

BRIEF IN SUPPORT OF PETITION

POINT I.

THE ALLEGED DISRATING OF NOIRMOT WAS VOID.

Maclachlan's Law of Merchant Shipping (6th Ed.) page 170, lays down the long accepted principle that:

> "It is obvious that a seaman who has faithfully performed his service on board, during the whole period of the intended voyage, is entitled to receive the whole of the stipulated reward. By the maritime law that reward is not to be diminished in consequence of the seaman's inability to render the stipulated service, if such inability has proceeded from any hurt received in the performance of his duty, or from natural sickness happening to him in the course of the voyage."

And it is submitted that when His Honor, Judge Waddill, —after deciding that:

> "While the right of a Master to demote a seaman, especially in a harbor, in the absence of the approval of the Consul of the ship's Country may be questioned" (R 81)

[which proposition was shown to be the law in *Butler v. Pacific* (CCA 9) 290 Fed. 806, where the Court said:

> "If the disrating occur at sea, the seaman disrated may claim his discharge as soon as the vessel reaches port, and if the *disrating occurs in port,* he may claim his *discharge forthwith,* and is *not bound* to accept the new position." (Italics mine.)] See also 9 *Fed. Stat. Anno.* 203-6 and cases cited; *Mattes v. Standard,* 274 Fed. 1019; *The Babcock* (CCA 2)

85 Fed. 978.; *Davidson v. U. S.* 1925 *A. M. C.* 1210; *The Ellen Little,* 246 Fed. 151.

—further held that:

> "still what was done here was reasonable, taking into account the fact that the mate had been injured, and the Master had to take that condition into account along with the others,"

a clear error was made (R 17, 20, 24-29, 38-40, 45-47, 56-59, 61, 68-69.)

In the first place the respondents gave no indication in the answers filed that Noirmot had been disrated, neither did Captain Burbidge lay any stress on it during his direct examination (R 20) his proctor going so far as to object to any cross-examination on this issue, contending that it was irrevelant (R 24) nor as held by the learned Court below, was there any effort on the part of the Master to seek an *adjudication* before the Consul at St. Johns (R 26, 56, 57, 81) or to comply with the statutes relating to the manner in which such matters should be determined and regarding the appropriate entries that must be made in the ship's Log Book (pp. 1, 4 & 18 of Exhibit W. L. B. No. 5) R. S. 4290, et seq, R. S. 4550, and R. S. 4597. The record discloses that the right to disrate was *flatly asserted* on the ground of Noirmot's alleged incompetency, and as this issue was determined in Noirmot's favor (R 57), when Judge Waddill found said contention untenable, and held that: "I don't see why he (the Master) should go through that sort of thing", and added, "I don't think it is material anyhow", to which respondent's proctor replied: "Depending on it was this man being disrated or not being disrated," it is submitted that no other excuse can be availed of by respondents (R 34), but in any event the alleged demotion would have been invalid because of the *Master's refusal* to pay Noirmot off on his demand (R 20, 33) after the purported disrating took place in the safe harbor of St. Johns. The bona fides of Captain Burbidge's conduct may be accurately judged by his forcing Noirmot to remain on board, for the convenience of the vessel, after he had endeavored to coerce Noirmot into accepting second mate's wages, three days later attempting to disrate him (R 25), and then forfeit two days wages because Noirmot went to see the Consul (R 47, 58), after being chased off the ship. Indeed under R. S. 4550, *supra*, in order to insist on a *valid* demotion, or the purported forfeitures hereinafter discussed, it was the *mandatory* duty of respondents to follow the plain terms of said statute which provides:

> "Every master shall, not less than forty-eight hours before paying off or discharging any seaman, *deliver* to him, or if he is to be discharged before a shipping-commissioner, to such shipping-commissioner, a *full* and *true account of his wages*, and *all deductions* to be made therefrom *on any account whatsoever;* and in default shall, for each offense, be liable to a penalty of not more than fifty dollars. *No deduction* from the wages of any seaman except in respect of some matter happening after such delivery *shall be allowed, unless it is included in the account delivered;* and the master *shall, during the voyage, enter* the various *matters* in respect to which such deductions are made, with the *amounts* of the *respective deductions as they occur,* in the official log-book * * * *." (Italics mine.)

and the record shows that *no effort* was made to comply with *any* of the applicable statutes.

POINT II.

THE ALLEGED FORFEITURES WERE ILLEGALLY DEDUCTED BY THE RESPONDENTS.

Deductions were made in the Log Book (pp. 18, 32 & 34 of Exhibit W. L. B. No. 5, *supra*), of forfeitures alleged against Noirmot and Derrane, yet there is no mention in the answers of any such claims, nor is any allegation made in the record regarding the *amounts* of the *purported penalties,* which were deducted from the wages of these men, in spite of the *actual waiver* as to Noirmot (R 25), and the legal waiver as to both, under the authorities. The Master admitted that the log entries involving Noirmot (for going to see the Consul at St. Johns, with the Master's permission, about getting paid off (R 25-27), were not proper (R 27), and said nothing whatever concerning why $8.00 was subtracted from Derrane's wages for ostensible forfeitures when no charges were even listed in the portion of the Log Book (pp. 4-29 of Exhibit W. L. B. No. 5) *supra,* provided therefor.

This Court made it plain in *Tucker v. Alexandroff,* 183 U. S. 424, at 443, that forfeitures may be imposed *only*: 'if the Master *shall* make a *proper* entry in the log book' (Italics mine). *Gordon v. U. S.,* 298 Fed. 555 *emphasizes* the same view and is the latest authority on the subject.

Keeping this requirement in mind the evidence leaves no room for doubt that the forfeitures sought to be imposed herein cannot be justified, under any circumstances, the purported entries in the log book making it evident that the law was disregarded in every respect. It is submitted that the trial court manifestly erred when it failed to make *any* finding whatever on this issue.

See R. S. 4550, *supra,* 4596-7 & 4600, 4603-5, 4610, and cases cited in 9 *Fed. Stat. Anno.,* at pp 203-209; 215-29. And see Mr. Justice Story's opinion in *U. S. v. Freeman,* Fed. Cas. No. 15, 162; *The Cora F. Cressy,* 131 Fed. 144; *The St. Paul,* 133 Fed. 1002; *The Ellen Little,* 246 Fed. 151, *supra; The Elizabeth Maersk,* 258 Fed. 765; 35 *CYC.* 1217, et seq, & 1226-7 and cases cited.

Forfeitures exacted of seamen, the 'wards of admiralty,' must conform strictly to the letter of R. S. 4550, 4596-7 and R. S. 4290, et seq, *supra,* inasmuch as violations of R. S. 4596, *supra,* are *misdemeanors, Hamilton v. U. S.,* 268 Fed 15, and this being true the respondents were obliged to furnish Noirmot and Derrane with definite information of the nature and cause of the accusations, confront them with their accusers, and *prove the alleged misdemeanors beyond a reasonable doubt,* and last, *but not least,* make the *required log entries.*

See 5th *and* 6th *Amendments to the U. S. Constitution; Maclachlan, supra,* p. 152 & 183.

Respondents did not contend in the trial court that any mutual releases were executed (R 21, 66) under R. S. 4552, nor did the said court so find (R 62-64), but even if such releases had been perfected, in connection with the amounts pocketed by said respondents on account of the alleged disrating and the forfeitures claimed, R. S. 4604, in addition to the monetary savings which accrued to them by reason of their wilful failure to comply with the Ship's Articles, (Exhibit W. L. B. No. 7) and R. S. 4612 respecting the proper kind and quantity of food that they were required to furnish petitioners, which issue is more fully discussed under Point IV. of this brief, they would have to be set aside in view of R. S. 4530.

> See *The Ellen Little, supra;* and *Pacific Mail v. Lucas,* 258 U. S. 266; *The Donna Lane,* 299 Fed. 977, construing R. S. 4530, *supra;* and also see Judge Rose's discussion in *Jones v. U. S.,* 284 Fed. 721, concerning seamen's releases in general.

POINT III.
THE SO-CALLED TENDER IS NO DEFENSE.

The Master refused, at the end of the voyage, to pay Noirmot off under protest (R 29, 61) and merely paid him one-third of the amount admittedly due, which should have been paid on October 22nd, 1924, under R. S. 4529, (R 27), and then left this one-third, in care of the Shipping Commissioner, only after specific demand was made therefor on October 23rd, 1924 (R 61-62). Late in the afternoon of that day and subsequent to the airing of the controversy before the Commissioner, the sum of $88.15 was deposited, over the petitioner's objection (R 21, 66), with the said Commissioner, but not until he agreed in writing to abide by the Master's instructions *not to pay it over* to Noirmot unless said petitioner signed off, in the release book, *without the right of protest* (R 28-29; 61-62; 66-67, Exhibits W. L. B. No. 2 & 3), and no move was made to permit Noirmot to receive this money *unconditionally* (see the trial Court's opinion, R 80-81) until January 5th, 1925 (R 10), when the $88.15 was deposited with the Clerk of the District Court by the respondents and the amended answer filed, without making any effort to take care of the accrued costs, which were later taxed at $232.74. On January 9th, 1925, Judge Waddill decreed said money to be due Noirmot and entered the order directing that it be paid to him without prejudice to the claims theretofore asserted by him and the other petitioners, so it appears that for eighty days Noirmot was forced to go without the wages which the respondents concede were due him, and under the authorities, there can be no tenable assertion by said respondents that this so-called tender is available to them as a defense herein.

> See *Mandelin v. Kenneally*, (CCA 4) 1926 A. M. C. ....; 10 F. (2d)............, *infra*, wherein Judge Waddill delivered the opinion of the Circuit Court of Appeals; *The Elizabeth Maersk, supra*; *Boulton v. Moore*, 14 Fed. 922; *Gerber v. Spencer*, 278 Fed. 886 (CCA 9); *Benedict's Admiralty*, (5 Ed.) Sec. 441; 26 *R. C. L.* 659.

The *Pacific Mail* and *Donna Lane* cases, *supra*, further demonstrate that the failure of the Master (R 29, 51), to give a seaman the certificate of discharge required by R. S. 4551, is deemed an important factor in subsequent controversies arising between them.

POINT IV.

EXTRA WAGES ARE DUE LIBELLANTS, UNDER R. S. 4568, BY REASON OF RESPONDENTS' FAILURE TO FURNISH THE QUANTITY AND QUALITY OF FOOD REQUIRED.

The Emma F. Angell, 217 Fed. 311, and *The Silver Shell*, 255 Fed. 340, show the law to be that the burden of proof on this issue is placed squarely on respondents, and His Honor, Judge Waddill, during the course of the trial (R 49, 51, 64), found that petitioners had not been furnished with the quality, (R 48-49), and quantity of food required by the Ship's Articles (p. 1 of Exhibit W. L. B. No. 7) and R. S. 4612 (R 51, 62, 64), but it appears from the learned Judge's opinion that he evidently concluded that the petitioners had waived their rights under the above Statutes (R 8-82). It is earnestly insisted that while under the authorities the petitioners *did not have to make any showing* that complaints had been made during the course of the voyage, such complaints were shown to have been brought home to the Master and Steward by far more than a fair preponderance of the evidence (R 12-14, 16-18, 22, 29-30, 34, 51, 63-64, 67-68). Indeed the Steward admitted to the Shipping Commissioner (Exhibit E) in the Master's presence, that *there had been* a shortage of fresh meats and vegetables. It is significant that, *without notice* to petitioners, the Steward was discharged on the very day the libel was filed (R 1, 31-33, 50, 66), and the Master made no effort to locate him thereafter.

It is submitted that complaints in this case, just as in *Billings v. Bauback, infra,* would have been superfluous, as Captain Burbidge conceded before the Commissioner and in the trial court that there was a shortage for the period in question (R 8, 22, 29-33, 64-66), and offered to pay all of the petitioners, with the exception of Noirmot $5.00 each on account of the food controversy (R 27, 32), though he asserts that he was willing to leave it to the Commissioner to pass on the amount due on this account. Yet, when the said Commissioner (Exhibit E) recommended the payment of $19.50 (R 14, 65) to each of petitioners in settlement of the food claims, the Master declined to pay these amounts and merely said he would pay all except Noirmot the $5.00 above mentioned, but assured the Commissioner and proctor for said petitioners, in the latters' presence (R 32), that he would immediately take these claims up with his owner in New York and advise them what the respondents would do with reference thereto without delay (R 30).

Billings v. Bauback, (CCA 9) 200 Fed. 523, is on all fours with the case at bar and is authority for the proposition that the petitioners were *not required,* under the circumstances, to make *any complaint* of the bad quality and insufficient quantity of food furnished them. In that case the learned Court held:—

> "The primary right of the seaman is to have provisions as called for by the scale. The law was plainly enacted for the purpose of assuring to the seaman a kind and quality of food well adapted for the preservation of his health, and the requirements of a seaman's life. But he may choose to accept such fare as the master may provide. The duty of the master, therefore, is to provide in accordance with the schedule, unless the seaman elects to accept the fare the master may provide. However, before the seaman can exercise an option as between the fare provided by the master and that included within the scale of provisions fixed by the statute, he *must have opportunity* of *selecting* an alternative diet; that is to say, the option *can be exercised only* where it can be fairly said *the seaman* has *had an opportunity for choice.*
>
> "Under the evidence in the record, the libellants herein never were offered any choice. Nothing was

ever said to them about such a thing. They *had no option*, nor *an opportunity* to *make effective a formal* demand for the government schedule. *The articles called for in the government schedule were not on the ship.* The Master, of course *knew* this; hence *a formal demand would have availed nothing.* * * * Under the circumstances it would be very unjust to hold that the seamen, by eating such as *they could* of the food provided by the master, exercised the option to accept it. *The real situation simply required libellants to accept what was provided by the master or go without food.*

With reference to the release interposed as a defense, the Court, *in accord* with Judge Waddill's views herein (R 62-66), said:

"The error of appellant's argument is in regarding the release involved as extending beyond wages, properly due to those who signed for their services on the voyage. There is no reference whatsoever in the release to claims on account of *reduction of allowance of provisions* or for *bad quality of food;* and, although claims for such compensation to which seamen are entitled are recoverable *as wages,* still they are not compensation for services on board a vessel, but, as expressly defined, are *allowances* by way of *compensation* to be paid *in addition to* wages." (Italics mine).

Nelson v. Patsel, (CCA 9) 232 Fed. 682, indicates the measure of *extra-wages* due on this branch of petitioners' claims, and it is submitted that the record here, including the findings of the trial Court thereon (R 13, 65, 81-82), entitles them to an award, under R. S. 4568, *supra,* based on practically all of the items embraced in R. S. 4612, *supra,* and the Ship's Articles (Exhibit W. L. B. No. 7), as with the exception of salt meat, bad flour, several rations of

salt fish, fresh meat on three occasions, and potatoes, on-
ions, carrots, parsnips and tomatoes a few times (R 13-14,
16-18, 49-51, 59-61, 63-66, 67-68) (some of these items were
uncertain in *both quantity* and *quality*) the respondents
have failed to establish that they have even partially com-
plied with the *duty imposed on them* thereunder. As point-
ed out in the above citation:—

> "The statute provides that the allowances attach
> to the reduction in any of the articles of food men-
> tioned in the scale from the quantities specified, and
> not a reduction in the *aggregate* of the daily allow-
> ances. *The purpose of the statute was plainly to
> require a variety of food and its allowance on certain
> days of the week as well as the quantity of the arti-
> cles of food therein specified.* The wording of the
> statute with its specification of allowable substitutes
> seems to us conclusive of this question. A specified
> article of *food cannot be withheld without furnishing
> a specified substitute,* and hence the *allowance must
> attach to a reduction in each article of food required,*
> and not to an aggregate reduction.

> "It is next contended by the respondent that, *hav-
> ing asked* Swanson, the cook, to furnish the respon-
> dent with a list of provisions required for the voy-
> age, the *latter had discharged* his duty to the libel-
> lants when provisions had been furnished in accord-
> ance with the list. The testimony about this list is
> not clear; but we do not think the fact, if established,
> is material, *The provisions furnished for the voy-
> age whether in accordance with the cook's list or not,
> were insufficient to serve the crew with the quantity
> of provisions provided in the statute.* There was a
> reduction in the provisions furnished, and *that is the
> test* of the *respondent's liability.*

> "The *agreement* of the master was that he would
> supply the crew with provisions *in accordance* with
> the schedule annexed to *Section* 4612 of the Revised

Statutes. This was a *positive* agreement, made in accordance with the *mandatory* terms of the statute

* * * * * * * * * * * *

"The statute is clearly *mandatory* and is designed to secure for each seaman a timely and suitable quantity, quality, and variety of food for the service for which he has been employed. *If there has been no failure* on the part of *master, shipowner, or charterer to comply* with the statute in this respect, it can be *easily established by proof*, and the court *need not be left in any doubt* upon the subject." (All but the first two italics mine).

Again, in *Thompson v. Martin*, 16 App. Cas. (D. C.) 222, with regard to the method used by the Courts to assess the amount of compensation due seamen under these statutes, it was held:—

"Proof of substantial failure to observe the requirements of the law with such reasonable particularity as to the number of days as will enable the court to assess the compensation with reasonable certainty is all that is necessary, without showing a failure from day to day, especially when the master and the owner knew of the scale in effect at the time and the seamen did not."

See 9*Fed. Stat. Anno.* 191-5,and cases cited; *Maclachlan, supra*, pp. 193-4; *Vincent v. U. S.* (CCA 9) 272 Fed. 889, *infra; Stewart v. U. S.*, etc., 7 F. (2d) 676, at 679.

It is pertinent here to note that neither Commissioner Wiatt (R 67), nor Derrane (R 69), both of whom gave *important testimony* in favor of the petitioners, were cross-examined, though the Commissioner was originally called as a witness for respondents (R 19).

It is submitted that the denial, herein, of *any* statutory allowance, for the food *admittedly short,* is untenable, and in open conflict with the *unbroken* line of *appellate* decisions, *supra,* none of which was distinguished by the learned Courts below. Even if it could be properly held that the penalty of double wages, provided under R. S. 4529, should not be imposed for the failure to pay the *extra wages,* due under R. S. 4568, *infra,* obviously the lower Courts erred, when they, in effect, held (R 81-82, 96) that the *mere* claiming of such double wages worked a *forfeiture* of the amounts properly due for shortage of food. R. S. 4568 provides that if the allowance of provisions is: "reduced * * * ;

> or if it shall be shown that any of such provisions are, or have been during the voyage, bad in quality or unfit for use, the seaman shall receive, by way of *compensation* for such reduction or bad quality, according to the time of its continuance, the following sums, to be *paid him in addition* to and to be *recoverable as wages*: (Italics mine)
>
> First. If his allowance is reduced by any quantity not exceeding one-third of the quantity specified by law, a sum not exceeding fifty cents a day.
>
> Second. If his allowance is reduced by more than one-third of such quantity, a sum not exceeding one dollar a day.
>
> Third. In respect of bad quality, a sum not exceeding one dollar a day. * * * * * *

Manifestly the facts disclosed in the instant case and *found* by the trial judge (R 49-51, 64, 67), require this Court to make it clear, in the language of *Thompson v. Martin, supra,* and in accord with the great weight of authority, that:—

"This law is *remedial,* and was enacted for a *bene-ficient* purpose, and while not to be enforced with undue severity should nevertheless, be *construed liberally,* so as to give its *humane* purpose *full* and *practical* effect, and cause it to be *respected* and *obeyed* by shipowners and masters." (Italics mine).

POINT V.

'WAITING TIME' IS DUE NOIRMOT FOR THE WAGES WITHHELD WITHOUT CAUSE.

The lower courts (R 81, 96) erred in holding, as a matter of law, that Noirmot's right to recover the indemnity provided by R. S. 4529 for withholding wages without sufficient cause, was affected by the $200.00 allowed him for the respondents' failure to furnish medical treatment or cure and the loss of time incident thereto, especially where *no unconditional offer* to pay same has ever been made (R 83-4), as pursuant to the above statute he became entitled, under the undisputed testimony (R 29, 61-62, 66), to two days pay for every day that elapses up to the time that the full amount of his wages, without any deductions on account of the attempted disrating or the forfeiture alleged, in addition to the indemnities sued for, and the costs incurred in his efforts to enforce collection thereof,—are entirely paid. The $88.15 adjudged to be due him was not forthcoming until after the entrance of the order of January 9, 1925 (R 11), eighty days subsequent to the time that it was admittedly payable. The costs of $232.74 were left unpaid, until *after* the order of March 23, 1925 (R 83), was entered, and it is submitted that at that time, in addition to $31.73 balance due for earned wages, 'waiting time' amounting to $810.67 had accrued to him, under the plain terms of the above statute, and that said 'waiting time' is subject to an increase of $5.33 for every day that said sums remain unpaid.

The following pronouncement of Judges Rose, Waddill and Parker in *The Roxen*, decided *January 14,1926*, 1926 A. M. C._____; 10 F (2d)_____, in which certiorari is likewise being applied for (R 103), is peculiarly opposite here: .

> "The Courts should act promptly and vigorously to vindicate all the rights of seamen as well those recently conferred on them as those which date from time immemorial. We doubt not that even now they will often need all the protection which can be given them."

In *Mandelin v. Kenneally*, 1926 A. M. C._____; 10 F. (2d)_____, *supra,* Judge Waddill, when handing down the opinion of the same court, then composed of Judges Waddill, Parker and McDowell, said:

> "Assignments 4 and 5 present the question of the right of the respondent to withhold the amounts admittedly due libellants at the end of their voyage on the 15th of November, 1924, at Newport News, Virginia, unless libellants would accept the same *upon the conditions imposed* by respondent. This the respondent *could not do*, as it constituted *neither a payment* of the wages nor a *lawful tender* of the amount due, but on the contrary, a *proffer* of a *future law suit* respecting the same. The fact that, in the litigation that followed in this particular case, the court sustained respondent's claim to withhold the fines and penalties imposed, would not warrant the *imposition* of any *such condition*·or penalty as was sought to be imposed. The only effect of libel-

lant's accepting the payment of the wages upon the conditions prescribed would have been to surrender their claims entirely. Under the law libellants were entitled to have paid them within two days after the termination of the voyage the amount of wages due them, and in default of such payment, Sections 4529-4530 of the Revised Statutes as amended by the Seamen's Act of March 4, 1915, 38 Stat. 1164, (Comp. Stat. 1916, Sects. 8320-22) imposed a penalty of two days' pay for each day of delay in payment. If this *important provision* of the statute looking to securing for seamen the *prompt* payment of wages due them could be lightly avoided by the *ship's prescribing conditions* like those in this case, it would work an *easy avoidance* of a *most important provision* of the law enacted for the *protection of seamen.* (Italics mine).

' * * * The mariners of a ship are commonly said to be wards of the admiralty. Their wages, their rights, their wrongs and injuries have always been a special subject of the admiralty jurisdiction.' * * *Benedict's Admiralty,* (4th Ed.) Section 182.

Gerber et als v. Spencer et als, 278 Fed. 886, 889-90 (CCA 9th Circuit), and cases cited.

The libellants are entitled to recover double wages at the rate of $60.00 per month for each day their wages were withheld, that is, from the 17th of November, 1924, to the first of January, 1925, inclusive, aggregating $720.00, the same to be distributed equally between the libellants, with costs. The judgment of the lower court will be accordingly modified and affirmed.''

Covert v. Wexford, 3 Fed. 577; *City of Montgomery,* 210 Fed. 673; *Pacific Mail v. Schmidt,* 241 U. S. 245; *Burns v. Davis,* (CCA 1) 271 Fed. 439; *Vincent v. U. S.* (CCA 9) 272 Fed. 889; *Gerber v. Spencer, supra; Nika,* 287 Fed. 717; *Great Canton,* 299 Fed. 953; *Morning Star,* 1 F. (2d) 410.

From these cases it will be seen that if separate actions had been instituted by Noirmot, the amount awarded him by the trial court for personal injuries and the *negligent failure* to provide him with medical attention and cure, could not, especially in view of his election to proceed under Section 33 of the "Merchant Marine Act" of June 5th, 1920, as construed in *Panama v. Johnson*, 264 U. S. 374, *supra* (R 3), affect respondent's liability for the wages and indemnities sued for herein. Distinct causes of action are set up in the libel and Noirmot is entitled to have each of his claims considered *separately* and on their own individual merits, *without prejudice* to one another. See *The C. S. Holmes*, (CCA 9) 237 Fed. 785, wherein the matter is succinctly treated and the ruling authorities carefully reviewed. Also *Gilfillan v. McKee*, 159 U. S. 302; *The Rolph* (CCA 9) 299 Fed. 52; *Morris v. U. S.* (CCA 2) 3 F. (2d) 588; *U. S. v. O'Shea* (App. D. C.) 5 F. (2d) 123; *Baltimore v. Phillips*, (CCA 2) 9 F. (2d) 902; *The Michael Tracy*, (CCA 4) 295 Fed. 680.

POINT VI.

'WAITING TIME' IS DUE *ALL* THE PETITIONERS FOR FAILURE TO PAY FOOD CLAIMS.

The amounts recommended to be paid to all of the petitioners, on account of the food claims, by the Shipping Commissioner (R 12, 14, 17, 18, 29, 49, 64, 65), in whose judgment the Master professed he was willing to abide, (R 28-29), were pitifully small, and far out of proportion to the allowances due them under R. S. 4568, as defined in

Nelson v. Patsel, supra, but nevertheless when the Master concedes that a *shortage existed* (R 8, 13, 16, 17, 18, 21, 22, 30, 32, 33, 49, 51, 63, 64, 65, 67, 68), there can be no escape from the fact that *some* allowance was due, and the mere offer to pay $5.00 to all the petitioners (R 27, 32), except Noirmot, in no way relieved respondents from paying the *proper* amount due *each of said petitioners* on their food claims, which, as we have seen, are recoverable as *extra wages,* and when we find that no effort has ever been made to properly settle any of the claims asserted for wages or extra-wages (R 8, 10, 30-33, 65-6, 83-84), (See District Court's opinion, R 80-81), the indemnities imposed under R. S. 4529 must follow.

CONCLUSION

The discussion, *supra,* discloses that at least twenty highly remedial Statutes are *necessarily* involved in a proper determination of this case. The opinions below do not discuss *any* of these enactments, nor is *any* case cited in support of the conclusions reached.

It is respectfully submitted that the applicable decisions of this Court and the great weight of authority are in accord with the views herein contended for, and that the questions involved are of sufficient general, material and national importance as to make it desirable that they be passed upon by this Honorable Court.

JACOB LOUIS MOREWITZ,
Proctor for Libellants-Petitioners.

CPSIA information can be obtained at www.ICGtesting.com
Printed in the USA
BVOW01s1039221014

371886BV00016B/302/P